W9-AGC-452

THE Little BOAT That Almost Sank

Matthew 14:22-33
Mark 6:45-51

FOR CHILDREN

Written by Mary Warren
Illustrated by Kveta Rada

"I am tired," said Jesus
to His friends one evening.

ARCH Books
© 1965 CONCORDIA PUBLISHING HOUSE, ST. LOUIS, MISSOURI
LIBRARY OF CONGRESS CATALOG CARD NO. 64-23371
MANUFACTURED IN THE UNITED STATES OF AMERICA
ALL RIGHTS RESERVED   ISBN 0-570-06010-9

"I will send the crowds away,
and then I must go into the hills alone
to talk to God.
You men row across the lake in your boat,
and I will meet you after a while."

The sun had set
like an enormous red balloon

floating down to the edge of the sky.

And now the birds tucked their heads
under their wings to sleep;

and the flowers folded themselves
quietly for the night;
and the stars prickled their sparkly way
into the great, black blanket of night.

Peter raised his hands in prayer.

"I will shove the boat off,"
said James to his friends
as they took up the oars.

The only sound was the soft sound
of wind whooshing the waves
and the soft slap of oars dipping in water.

"The wind is getting worse," said John after they had rowed for a bit.
"We want to make our boat go one way, but the wind is starting
to push it the other way."

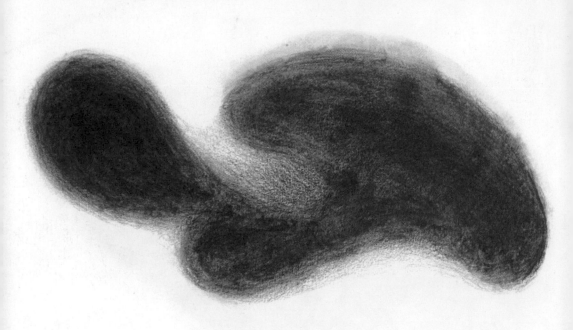

By then the sound of the wind had become
like the roar of an angry lion.
The little waves turned to big waves,
and the big waves
thumped and bumped and rocked the boat
and splashed water into it.

"I'm scared!" shouted Andrew
above the noise of the wind
and the boom of the waves.

"I am a fisherman
and have been in rough water many times.
But this is terrible! I'm scared!"

"I am, too!" shouted Peter.
"If Jesus were here, I would not feel so scared."

"I wish He had come with us!"
called another man, wet and trembling
and afraid.

When Jesus looked out from the top of the hill,
He could see the boat rocking in the moonlight
and all of the men pulling hard at the oars.

"That is a strong wind!" He said to Himself.
"It is the middle of the night,
and they are getting nowhere.
They must be wet and cold and frightened."

Down the hill went Jesus,
down the hill and over the rocks,
down in the dark

until He got to the shore.

The wind hissed and the waves roared
and the boat rocked and the men trembled —
afraid!

Then they saw Jesus —
walking toward them on the water!
They were stiff with fear.
"A ghost!" they screamed.
"The storm is bad enough.
But now — a ghost!"

But over the hiss of the wind
and the boom of the waves
and the cries of the men
came a voice they knew:
"It is I! Do not be afraid!"

"O Jesus! Jesus!" called Peter,
"If that is really You, please tell me
to come to You on the water!"

In the darkness, above the roar of the wind,
Jesus said quietly: "Come, Peter! Come!"

Peter climbed over the side of the boat
and, looking ahead at Jesus, he felt brave.
He took some steps out on the water,
but suddenly the waves thundered in his ears,
and instead of looking at Jesus, he looked down.

"I cannot do it!" he thought to himself,
and he began to sink.
"Lord! Help!" he cried.
Jesus quickly stretched His arm and caught him.
"Peter! Peter!
You thought you could not do it?
Why don't you have more faith in Me?"

Together they climbed into the boat.
The wind stopped roaring
and the waves stopped pounding
and the boat stopped rocking,
and there came again
the gentle whoosh of the waves
and the soft slap of the oars
dipping in water.

"Jesus!"
whispered Peter and Andrew and all of the men.
"You can make a storm go away!
You can make the winds hush!
When You are with us,
we are not afraid."

Dear Parents:

This story is a story of awe and wonder over the mysterious and kingly power of the Lord Christ: "Who is He whom even the waves and winds obey?"

To the people of the Bible, much more exposed to the mercy of the elements than our city man of today, the "waters" and the wind were not just uncontrollable; they were also mysterious and often frightening. When describing the greatness of God's power, they loved to picture Him as mastering the water and the wind — driving them, blowing, walking, sitting, riding upon them — or rescuing His people from them (e.g., Exodus 14:21, 22; 15:8-11; Psalm 18:6-19; 29; 77:14-19). He who is more powerful than the elements is the Master of the universe and the Saviour of His people. He is stronger than all the forces that would do us harm. There is no need to lose heart when He is near.

Peter sensed this and ventured out toward his Lord outside the boat. But then he made a mistake we all do. Instead of looking at his Lord he was distracted by the strong wind. He lost his nerve and the "ground" under his feet. But Jesus did not let him sink.

Will you help your child think of Jesus as this story pictures Him?

THE EDITOR